What people are saying about "Not the Bible"

Your best laugh now.
Joel Osteen*

          The perfect indulgence.
                    Johann Tetzel*

Russia denies meddling in the funniness of this book.
Vladimir Putin*

        It's my unbiased opinion that this is the best book I've ever read.
                             John's mum

---

* Everything's true about these statements except the quotes.

More NOT THE PARABLES OF JESUS

Other books by the author

The Lost Parables Series
The Donkey and the King
Ana and the Prince
The Princess and the Crocodile

Not the Bible Titles
Not the Parables of Jesus
More Not the Parables of Jesus
Not the Parable of the Good Samaritan
Still More Not the Parables of Jesus
Not the Parable of the Lost Sheep (free for subscribers)
Not the Parable of the Rich Fool (subscribers only)
Not the Christmas Story Vol 1 (with devotional)

Christian Parody Titles
Not the Love Dare
Not the Christmas Story: A Comedic Christmas Caper

Christian Satirical News
The Best of the Salty Cee Vol 1

Satirical Publishing Titles
Get 1,000 Readers for Your Self-Published Book

More NOT THE PARABLES OF JESUS

Revised Satirical Version (RSV)

John Spencer

More Not the Parables of Jesus

Copyright © 2018 John Spencer.

All rights reserved. No part of this book may be copied or reprinted for commercial gain. However, these stories are meant to be shared, used as skits, sermon illustrations, stories for Sunday school or for small group discussion. Individual parables may be reproduced for these purposes, but please honour the effort that went into writing them by referencing their source. For other uses please obtain written permission from the author via his website www.johnspencerwrites.com.

Unless otherwise quoted, all "Not the Bible" quotations are taken from the Revised Satirical Version (RSV) © 2017.

Nothing in this book is intended as a substitute for the Bible. The reader should regularly consult a Bible in matters relating to his/her spiritual development and particularly with respect to any behaviour that may require truth.

I wonder if anyone actually reads this small print. Tell you what. If you are then send me an email with the subject "I'm OCD and read all the small print" and I'll send you a bonus ebook of 10 parables.

Published by:

Kingdom Collective Publishing

Unit 10936, PO Box 6945
London, W1A 6US
kingdomcollectivepublishing@gmail.com

Book and Cover idea by John Spencer, design by Akira007
Not the Bible icon – design by John Spencer, created by dalmatirac design studio
Editing by Katherine.
ISBN: 978-1-912045-52-5

First Edition: April 2018

Dedication

This one's for the Christian anon gang on Twitter.

Thank you for your welcome, your banter, your jokes, and for laughing at my gags, even if I did have to pay you.

CONTENTS

WHAT PEOPLE ARE SAYING ABOUT "NOT THE BIBLE" I
DEDICATION VII

NOT THE END 3

TRIGGER WARNING 5

NOT THE PARABLES 7

THE LOST SHEEP 9
THE PRODIGAL SON 10
PARABLE OF THE TALENTS 11
THE GOOD SAMARITAN 12
PARABLE OF THE MUSTARD SEED 13
THE WHEAT AND THE TARES 14
LABOURERS IN THE VINEYARD 16
THE SHEEP AND THE GOATS 18
THE PRODIGAL SON 2 20
THE PERSISTENT WIDOW 22
THE PEARL OF GREAT PRICE 23
THE GREAT BANQUET 24
THE RICH MAN AND LAZARUS 25
THE GOOD SAMARITAN 2 27
THE LOST SHEEP 2 28
THE HIDDEN TREASURE 29
THE PARABLE OF THE YEAST 30
THE PHARISEE AND THE TAX COLLECTOR 31
PARABLE OF THE TALENTS 2 33
THE PRODIGAL SON 3 35
THE TEN VIRGINS 37
THE LAMP ON A STAND 39
THE SHREWD MANAGER 40
THE WICKED TENANTS 41
THE GREAT BANQUET 2 42
THE LOST COIN 43
THE WEDDING GARMENT 44

    THE GOOD SAMARITAN 3 45
    THE UNFORGIVING SERVANT 46
    THE PRODIGAL SON 4 49
    PARABLE OF THE NET 50
    THE RICH FOOL 51
    PARABLE OF THE SOWER 52

PERFECT PARABLES 53

    THE PERSISTENT WIDOW 55
    THE PHARISEE AND THE TAX COLLECTOR 56
    THE TWO SONS 57
    THE WICKED TENANTS 58

POINTLESS PARABLES 59

    THE LAMP ON A STAND 61
    THE UNFORGIVING SERVANT 62
    THE PRODIGAL SON 63
    PARABLE OF THE TALENTS 65
    THE SHREWD MANAGER 66

THE LOST PARABLES 67

    THE BAND WHO DIDN'T PLAY 69

NOT THE BEGINNING 73

    GET BONUS CONTENT 75
    FEEDBACK 76
    ABOUT THE AUTHOR 77
    KEEP IN TOUCH 78
    OTHER BOOKS BY THE AUTHOR 80
    KINGDOM COLLECTIVE PUBLISHING 82

NOT
the End

A clever section title that makes it sound like it's more important than an introduction.

Hopefully, people might read it which may cut down on the number of angry emails I receive...

Trigger Warning

Please be aware that this book contains the following triggers:

English Spelling

Those who have been brought up spelling any way other than the English do may take offence at the appearance of 'u's in words that had previously lacked such magnificence. I encourage you to embrace your true mother tongue. Should this be too much, then I recommend the audio version of this book instead.

Parables

Those raised in a Western rational reductionist learning environment may take offence at the lack of truth expressed in a clearly explained "moral of the story". Please note: Jesus *is* the Truth and never explained the moral of the prodigal son. I encourage you to let the story speak to you on a deeper level than mere facts ever could. Should this be too alarming, I recommend you purchase a dry commentary on the parables instead.

Humour[1]

Those who have been told that laughter is of the devil, and the second fruit of the Spirit is sombreness, may take offence at the use of quirky British humour to open eyes to the lies we believe about God, ourselves, and the world. Please note: Jesus often used humour to expose false thinking (e.g. straining out a gnat and swallowing a camel.) I encourage you to let my humour do its job[2]. Should this prove too much, then I recommend composing a strongly worded complaint to me as you read this book.

Free Speech

Only joking. This book costs money[3].

---

[1] See trigger warning #1 above.

[2] And no, not just on the people/theology/politics/denominations you disagree with!

[3] If somehow you got it free then I recommend you refer to the eighth commandment.

N⊘T
the Parables

Different takes on the parables to restore the wonder, the joy of the Gospel and the discomfort of discovering what we really believe in our hearts.

Mt 18:12-14; Lk 15:4-7
The Lost Sheep

What do you think? If a man has one hundred sheep and one of them wanders away, will not the ninety-nine sheep say, 'We are the ninety-nine percent majority!' Will they not protest and lobby the shepherd to ensure he does not give preferential treatment to the one percent through spending the time and effort to bring them back?

Suppose then another sheep wanders off. Will not the ninety-eight sheep who remain say, 'We are the ninety-eight percent majority!' and protest so that the shepherd doesn't go after that sheep either.

And will not this trend continue until the remaining sheep realise their flock has shrunk, then turn on the shepherd for being so neglectful as to allow so many sheep to wander off?

Lk 15:11-32
The Prodigal Son

A man had two sons. The younger said to his father, 'Father, give me my share of the estate now, instead of making me wait until you die.' So the Father divided his property between them.

Soon after, the younger son packed all he had and set off for a distant country. But the son discovered that it was a magic bag that never ran out of money, so he lived happily ever after, gambling, drinking, and sleeping around.

Mt 25:14-30; Lk 19:11-27
Parable of the Talents

"The Kingdom of heaven is like a man going on a journey who called his servants together and entrusted his wealth to them. To the first, he gave one talent, to the second, two and to the third, five talents, each in proportion to his ability. Then he left on his journey.

The first servant immediately invested his one talent and gained one more. The second servant gained two talents more. But the last servant wrote books, then started a ministry about how God had blessed him with five talents. He made a tidy profit through his instructional material on how to receive five talents by being a good and faithful servant."

Lk 10:25-37
The Good Samaritan

Jesus replied, "There once was a man travelling from Jerusalem to Jericho who was attacked by robbers. They beat him, stripped him of his clothes and money then left him lying half dead beside the road.

Luckily, a Charismatic happened to be going down the same road. When he saw the man, he prayed in tongues, then continued on his way to a healing conference. So too, a Baptist came by, and when he saw the man, he quoted from the Bible that the Lord was the man's healer. He then continued on his way to preach to others in need.

Then a Facebook user came upon the man, saw him there and had compassion on him. He changed his profile picture to stand with those who are injured by robbers whilst travelling[5].

"Which of these three would you say was a neighbour to the man attacked by robbers?" The expert in the law replied, "All three." Jesus replied, "Go and do likewise."

---

[5] However, despite the post receiving over 1000 likes, the man still died.

Mt 13:31-32; Mk 4:30-32; Lk 13:18-19
Parable of the Mustard Seed

The Kingdom of Heaven is like a mustard seed that a man planted, and it grew into a small shrub. A man compared its size with other trees and thought, "There's no point doing anything with this until its bigger." So, he dismissed it. And because it was never tended to, it never grew any bigger.

Mt 13:24-30, 36-43
The Wheat and the Tares

Jesus told them this parable, "The Kingdom of Heaven is like a man who sowed good seed in his field. While he slept, his enemy came and sowed tares in the middle of the wheat. While the good seed grew, so did the weeds.

The servants saw this and came to him and said, 'Sir, wasn't that good seed that you sowed in the field? Where did all the weeds come from?'

He answered, 'A powerful enemy has done this.'

They responded, 'Shall we pull them up?'

'No, because the tares look like the wheat and you might mistakenly pull up wheat.'

But the weeds grew much faster than the wheat and soon dwarfed them. As a result, the wheat became stunted. The weeds blocked much of the sunlight and stole nearly all the water and nutrients from the ground.

The servants returned to their master and expressed their dismay, 'Surely we should pull up the weeds now! Look what they're doing to the crop!'

The master sighed, saying, 'The weeds' roots are intertwined with those of the wheat, so we cannot remove them without damaging the crop even more. You must allow both to grow until harvest time. Then shall the weeds be removed and burned.'

And so, at harvest time the servants did as their master commanded, throwing huge bundles of weeds into the flames. But the harvest was pitiful. It barely filled a bucket, let alone a barn."

Later, when the crowds were sent away, the disciples asked, "Explain to us the parable of the wheat and the tares."

Jesus answered, "The Son of Man sows the good seed. The field is the world. The good seed stands for the sons of the kingdom, and the tares are the children of the evil one. The enemy who sowed them is the devil. The harvest is the end of the age, and the harvesters are the angels.

"That is how it is going to be. Christians are going to be small and powerless in this dark world, and they'll have to hold on through it all until the end."

Mt 20:1-16
Labourers in the Vineyard

"The Kingdom of Heaven is like a vineyard owner who hired men to work in his vineyard. He agreed to pay them a denarius for a day's work.

At the third hour, he was in the market place and saw there were other men still waiting to be hired. He said, 'Come, work in my vineyard.' And so, they did.

The owner went out again several times that day and did the same thing. When there was only an hour left in the workday, he still found men standing around waiting to be hired. 'Let me guess; you've not been hired because you don't have the skills people are looking for?'

The men shrugged their shoulders as they recognised the truth being spoken about them. The owner sighed, 'Well, I suppose you'd better come and help me in my vineyard then.'

When the end of the day came, the owner instructed his foreman to pay the workers. 'Make sure you pay the ones who worked all day first. They have put in the most effort and were the best of the bunch I hired today.'

The workers who were hired at the eleventh hour received only a few pennies. They looked at their wages and shrugged; they understood that was all they were worth.

The first will get the glory, and the last will get the leftovers. Just as it is in this world, so it shall be in the Kingdom."

Mt 25:31-46
The Sheep and the Goats

When the Son of Man comes in all his blazing glory together with his angels, he shall sit on his glorious throne. And all the nations shall be gathered before him and he shall separate the people as a shepherd separates the sheep from the goats, putting the sheep to his right and goats to his left.

Then the King will say to those on his right, 'Come, blessed of my Father, take your inheritance - the Kingdom prepared for you from the world's foundation. For you led great ministries, you preached to thousands, you wrote books and became celebrities.'

Then the righteous will reply, 'Lord, we were pretty amazing, weren't we?'

Then the King will say to those on his left, 'Away with you, cursed ones, into the fires prepared for the devil and his demons since the world's foundation. For you had no huge ministries or followings, you wrote no books, you only loved your spouse and your children well and cared for the people you met.'

Then the unrighteous will reply, 'Lord, we know we had no

influence and did little in this world, therefore we deserve nothing special.'

Then they shall be herded to their eternal punishment, but the righteous to eternal life.

Lk 15:11-32
The Prodigal Son 2

A man had two sons. The younger said to his father, 'Father, give me my share of the estate now, instead of making me wait until you die.' So the Father divided his property between them.

Soon after, the younger son packed all he had and set off for a distant country. There he squandered his money in wild living until it was all gone. At that time, there was a great famine and he began to starve. The only job he could find was feeding a Gentile farmer's pigs. The boy became so hungry that he wanted to eat the pig swill.

When he finally came to his senses, he said, 'At home, even my father's servants have food to spare, and here I am starving to death! I will go home to my father and say, 'Father, I've sinned against God and against you. I am no longer worthy to be called your son. Take me on as a hired servant.'

And so, he got up and headed home to his father. When he reached home, his father met him at the door, and the son began his speech, 'Father, I have sinned against God and against you. I am no longer worthy to be called your son – '

But his father cut him off, saying angrily, 'What do you want? You've got some nerve coming back here. You took a third of my land, sold it, wasted the proceeds, and now you hope for more?' And he set the dogs on him.

Lk 18:1-8
The Persistent Widow

Jesus told his disciples a parable to show their need to be persistent in prayer if they want to get anywhere. He said, "There was a judge in a town who did not fear God nor did he care for people. A widow in that town kept at him, 'Grant me justice against my adversary.' At first, the judge ignored her, but eventually, she got on his nerves enough that he finally caved in.

'I might not fear God nor care for people, but if I don't give this woman justice she will drive me insane!'"

Then Jesus said, "So too will you have to nag and beg God before He will answer your prayers."

Mt 13:45-46
The Pearl of Great Price

The Kingdom of Heaven is like a man who discovered the most valuable pearl in the world. As he felt no other pearl compared to it, he felt it was his moral obligation to go around telling everyone else that their pearls were rubbish.

Mt 22:1-14; Lk 14:15-24
The Great Banquet

Once, there was a man who prepared a wedding banquet for his son and sent out many invitations. When all was ready, he sent his servant to inform the guests that it was time to come. But they all began to make excuses. The first said, 'I apologise, but I've just purchased a field that I need to inspect.'

Another said, 'I apologise, but I've just purchased five pairs of oxen that I need to try out.' Still another said, 'I am just married, so I need to get home to my wife.'

The servant reported all this to his master. His master was angry and told the servant, 'Quickly, go into the city streets and alleys and invite all the poor, dispossessed, crippled, and the blind and then bring them here.' But they were suspicious of the invitation and refused to come. After all, no one important ever invited them to a party before, why would they now?

The master was exasperated as he had no guests to attend his son's wedding. They either thought themselves as too important or as too unimportant to come.

Lk 16:19-31
The Rich Man and Lazarus

There once was a rich man who was splendidly dressed and lived in luxury every day. A poor, diseased beggar named Lazarus was laid at his door. He longed to eat whatever might fall from the rich man's table, and the dogs would come and lick his open sores.

Then the beggar died and was carried by the angels to be with Abraham. The rich man also died and was buried. He ended up in the fires of hell where he looked up and saw Abraham in the distance with Lazarus by his side.

He called out, 'Hi there, Lazarus! I'm currently in the fires of purification, but I'll join you shortly when this vast chasm that separates us is removed.'

The rich man then asked, 'Father Abraham, send Lazarus to my father's house, for I have five brothers. Let him warn them about this place of purification so they can go straight to heaven.'

But Abraham replied, 'There's no point, everyone will eventually end up here anyhow. It isn't worthwhile to warn people. It'll just make them fearful and reinforce the lies that evil leaders spread. This is the good news of the Gospel. Everyone that wants to be saved from the fires will be, just as it was in the days of the Great Flood.'

Lk 10:25-37
The Good Samaritan 2

Jesus replied, "There once was a man travelling from Jerusalem to Jericho who was attacked by robbers. They beat him, stripped him of his clothes and money then left him lying half dead beside the road.

Luckily, a priest happened to be going down the same road. But when he saw the man he crossed to the other side and walked past him. So too, a Levite came by. He also crossed to the other side to avoid the man.

Then a Samaritan came upon the man and saw how the previous two Jews had ignored the man. He shouted at them, 'You selfish people! That's typical of you Jews!' He then carried on his way.

Which of these three would you say was a neighbour to the man attacked by robbers?"

The expert in the law replied, "The one who shouted at the others."

Jesus replied, "Go and do likewise."

Mt 18:12-14; Lk 15:4-7
The Lost Sheep 2

What do you think? If a man has one hundred sheep and loses one of them, does he not leave the ninety-nine and go searching for it until he finds it? And when he finds it, doesn't he begrudgingly fling it over his shoulders to carry home, whilst giving it a stern lecture the whole way back? And won't he bring that incident up whenever that sheep does anything foolish in the future?

I tell you, in the same way, your Father in heaven will berate you and constantly bring up your past sins.

Mt 13:44
The Hidden Treasure

The Kingdom of Heaven is like a farmer who ploughed his field ready for planting. As he was doing so, the plough's blade slammed against a metal box full of treasure buried just below the surface.

The farmer looked at the bent plough blade and cursed the box of treasure, "Look what you've done! You've bent my plough and I'm going to have to waste time fixing this before I can finish my work!"

In anger he picked up the box and hurled it out of the field so that it wouldn't mess up his life again.

Mt 13:33; Lk 13:20-21
The Parable of the Yeast

The Kingdom of Heaven is like yeast which was so sure of its specialness that it kept itself separate from the bread. It then cursed the bread for not rising.

Lk 18:9-14
The Pharisee and the Tax Collector

Then he told this parable to everyone who was looked down upon by those who called themselves righteous.

"Two men went to the Temple to pray, one a Pharisee, the other a tax collector. The Pharisee prayed: 'God, I thank you that I'm not like everyone else, especially not that tax collector over there! For I fast twice a week and give a tenth of all my income.'

But the tax collector stood at a distance, his face in his hands, not daring to look up to Heaven and said, 'God have mercy on me, a sinner.'

People were incensed by the way the poor tax collector was victimised by the judgemental Pharisee. And so, they staged protests, boycotts, and riots until the law was changed to make it a crucifixion offense to judge others.

Now, because no one dared judge the tax-collectors, they continued their swindling ways and sold out their fellow countrymen to the occupying Romans without any fear of reprisal.

Two men went to the Temple to pray, one a Pharisee and the other a tax-collector. The tax-collector stood up and prayed, 'God, I thank you that I am not like other men who are bigoted, judgemental, and prideful like that Pharisee over there. I report those who post anything I find offensive and I close down synagogues that preach judgement against people like me.'

But the Pharisee stood at a distance. He would not even look up to heaven but beat his breast and said, 'God have mercy on me, a sinner.'

I tell you that the tax-collector rather than the Pharisee went home justified before God. For the humbled will be exalted and then humble their oppressors in turn. As they were once victims, their humbling of others will be considered righteous."

Mt 25:14-30; Lk 19:11-27
Parable of the Talents 2

"The Kingdom of heaven is like a man going on a journey who called his servants together and entrusted his wealth to them. To the first, he gave five talents, to the second, two talents and the third, one talent, each in proportion to his ability.

The first servant immediately invested his five talents and gained five more. The second servant gained two more. But the last servant said, 'There's no point investing what I've been entrusted with until I acquire more.' And so, the servant waited until his moment came! From out of nowhere, four more talents appeared before him. As he now had as many talents as the first servant, he invested them and earned five more.

After a long time, their master returned from his trip and called his servants to account for his investment. He saw what they had obtained and praised them, 'Well done good and faithful servants! You have been faithful with a few things, and so I will entrust you all with much more. Come and share your master's joy!'

So it will be for those who do not use their gifts until they are given great ministries."

Lk 15:11-32
The Prodigal Son 3

A man had two sons. The younger said to his father, 'Father, give me my share of the estate now, instead of making me wait until you die.' So the Father divided his property between them.

Soon after, the younger son packed all he had and set off for a distant country. There he squandered his money in wild living until it was all gone. At that time, there was a great famine and he began to starve. The only job he could find was feeding a Gentile farmer's pigs. The boy became so hungry that he wanted to eat the pig swill.

Soon, word of his situation reached his father's village and they were in uproar about the uncleanliness of the son's current occupation. The leaders of the community accosted the father, 'Your son has brought disgrace upon you and this whole community! You need to deal with him in the severest way possible so that this sinful behaviour is purged!'

The father responded calmly, 'It is your behaviour that brings disgrace by clinging to outdated laws. I couldn't be more proud of my son the pig-farmer. He has bravely embraced his true identity, regardless of your insults. He's my beloved son, therefore I accept and support his chosen lifestyle no matter what you may say or think.'

Mt 25:1-13
The Ten Virgins

"The Kingdom of Heaven is like ten girls who went out to meet the bridegroom. Five were wise and knew the bridegroom well as a result of spending much time with him. Five were foolish and only knew about him by what others said or by reading books about him. However, they still hoped to get into the wedding celebration.

Now the bridegroom and his wedding entourage were taking their time getting there, and the girls grew drowsy as they waited. They all fell asleep. At midnight, a shout arose, 'Here comes the bridegroom! Come and meet him!'

The girls awoke, trimmed their lamps, and joined the wedding procession. However, as they came to the house it became clear that the bridegroom was greeting people at the door by name. Since the foolish virgins did not know the bridegroom personally, he wouldn't know who they were and so they wouldn't be able to slip into the feast unnoticed. There's no way the bridegroom would let strangers into his feast.

The foolish girl's panic became obvious to the wise virgins, who graciously offered, 'Look, why don't we lend you some of our friendship with the bridegroom?'

The foolish virgins were so grateful, 'Thank you so much!'

And so, all the virgins were admitted, and none were turned away with the dreaded words: 'I don't know you.'

"Therefore, I tell you, don't worry about the bridegroom's return. Someone will help you enter into the celebration even if you don't bother to get to know him personally."

Mk 4:21-25; Lk 8:16-18
The Lamp on a Stand

Everyone lights a lamp and sets it upon a lamp stand so all can see. However, the darkness is difficult for the light to overcome and so it takes ages for the lamp to illuminate a dark room. So too will you struggle to overcome the darkness in your world.

Lk 16:1-12
The Shrewd Manager

Jesus told this story to his disciples, "There was a rich man who had a Christian manager who handled his affairs. However, he heard reports that the manager was doing a poor job. But he thought, 'That can't be true! I'd rather have a trustworthy Christian looking after my money than any unsaved person.'

However, the reports were actually accurate, and so over time, the rich man continued to lose money until he realised the problem. Not wanting to hurt his fellow brother in Christ, he resorted to passive aggressive techniques in the hopes the man would quit. His plan worked spectacularly well."

Jesus then said, "The Christians of this world are universally good at handling money and relationships. That's why working for a Christian company is always such a blessing. Therefore, Christians should be put in charge of much regardless of how well they handle little."

Mt:21:33-44; Mk 12:1-12; Lk 20:9-18
The Wicked Tenants

Jesus spoke to them in parables. "A man planted a vineyard. He put a wall around it, dug a pit for the winepress and built a watchman's tower. Then he leased it to some tenant farmers and went away. At harvest time, he sent a servant to collect his share of the crop.

They grabbed him, beat him, and sent him back empty-handed. The owner learned his lesson and hired a mob who then beat the tenants and kicked them off his land. New tenants were brought in to take the place of the old, and a great harvest was collected.

For in the Kingdom, God will give up on you, at the first sign of your disobedience, and replace you with another."

Mt 22:1-14; Lk 14:15-24
The Great Banquet 2

Once, there was a man who prepared a great banquet and then sent out many invitations to the noble and high-born. When all was ready, he sent his servant to inform the guests that it was time to come. They all came straight away, even those who just purchased fields and oxen and the ones who were just married.

The host was pleased that he didn't have to invite any of the poor, dispossessed, crippled, and the blind as they would have made the banquet an uncomfortable affair.

For few are invited and for a good reason too.

Lk 15:8-10
The Lost Coin

Suppose a woman has ten silver coins and loses one. Won't she think that it's only one coin that could easily be replaced? Won't she decide it's not worth the time and effort to look for it? So it is with God. If you're daft enough to get lost and wander away from Him, then you're on your own.

Mt 22:10-14
The Wedding Garment

The king said to his servants, 'The wedding banquet is ready, but those I invited weren't worthy. Therefore, go to the street corners and invite everybody you see.' So, the servants brought in anyone they could find; the good, the bad, and the ugly, until the wedding hall was full to the brim.

But when the King entered the hall, he noticed a man who wasn't wearing the wedding clothes provided for him. He asked, 'How dare you come to my son's wedding dressed like that!' The man replied, 'Given the people that you have invited, I thought you were accepting of all. This is who I am. Why should *I* have to wear your wedding clothes?'

The king retorted, 'Because this is a wedding! If who you are is someone who doesn't show respect to my son on his special day, then clearly you don't belong here!'

Enraged, the king instructed his servants, 'Bind him and throw him into the darkness where there is weeping and gnashing of teeth.'

For many are called and some believe they are chosen even if they don't intend on obeying the king.

Lk 10:25-37
The Good Samaritan 3

Jesus replied, "There once was a Samaritan travelling from Jerusalem to Jericho who was attacked by robbers. They beat him, stripped him of his clothes and money then left him lying half dead beside the road.

Luckily, a priest happened to be going down the same road. But when he saw the man he crossed to the other side, walking past him. So too, a Levite came by. He also crossed to the other side to avoid the man.

Then an everyday Jew came upon the man, saw him there and felt compassion for him. But when he noticed the man was a Samaritan, he continued on his journey.

Which of these three would you say was a neighbour to the man attacked by robbers?"

The expert in the law replied, "The one who had compassion on him."

Jesus replied, "Go and do likewise, but do no more than that man."

Mt 18:21-35
The Unforgiving Servant

Then Peter came to Jesus and asked, "Master, how many times should I forgive my brother who sins against me? Seven times?"

Jesus replied, "Peter, you should always say you forgive your brother, regardless of whether or not you mean it. God looks at the outward appearance.

The Kingdom of Heaven is like a king who decided to settle accounts with his servants. One of his servants who was brought before him owed seven billion dollars.

The servant couldn't possibly pay it back, so the king ordered the man, his wife, children, and all his belongings to be sold to repay the debt.

The man threw himself at the king's feet and begged, 'Be patient with me, and I'll pay it all back.' The king was impressed by the servant's grovelling as such behaviour proved that the groveler understood the king's rank. And so, the king released the servant, forgiving his debt based on his outstanding outward performance.

After the man left the king's chamber, he came upon one of his fellow servants who owed him 12,000 dollars. Grabbing his fellow servant by the throat, He demanded, 'Pay back what you owe me!'

His fellow servant threw himself at the man's feet and begged, 'Be patient with me, and I'll pay it all back.' The man said, 'I forgive you' then had the servant put in jail until the debt was repaid in full. When the other servants saw this, they were outraged and told the king everything.

The king replied to them, 'As I have witnessed this servant's humble posture in my presence, that's what counts. What he does outside of my court doesn't affect my relationship with him at all.' But the servants retorted, 'Surely his behaviour outside your court will call your benevolence into disrepute.' The king replied, 'On the contrary, my reputation will be even better when others compare his alleged actions to my benevolence.'

When the servant repeated his behaviour, the other servants didn't bother to tell the king. They just chalked it up to hypocrisy.

So too shall my Heavenly Father think highly of you if you are apologetic in his presence and appear humble and chaste during Sunday service. It doesn't matter to him how you behave outside of church services. After all, it's a dog-eat-dog world out there."

So, Peter kept up appearances by saying, "I forgive you" to his brother. He rejoiced in his freedom to hold on to his grudge.

Lk 15:11-32
The Prodigal Son 4

A man had two sons. The younger said to his father, 'Father, give me my share of the estate now, instead of making me wait until you die.' So the Father divided his property between them.

Soon after, the younger son packed all he had and set off for a distant country. There he squandered his money in wild living until it was all gone. At that time, there was a great famine and he began to starve. The only job he could find was feeding a Gentile farmer's pigs. The boy became so hungry that he wanted to eat the pig swill.

When he finally came to his senses, he said, 'At home, even my father's servants have food to spare, and here I am starving to death through my bad choices. Therefore, I am no longer worthy to be called my father's son and I deserve this miserable life.'

Mt 13:47-50
Parable of the Net

The Kingdom of Heaven is like a net which was cast into the sea and caught all kinds of things. When it was full, the fishermen hauled it to shore and kept everything as it would be unloving of them to throw anything away. Some of the fishermen's meals were toxic but such is the price of love.

So too will it be at the end of the age. The angels will come and let everyone into heaven.

Lk 12:16-21
The Rich Fool

"Beware! Be on your guard against all kinds of poverty mindset; life does not consist of the absence of riches."

Then he told them this parable: "The farm of a certain rich man produced an amazing crop. He thought to himself, 'Clearly this is the blessing of God! He wants me to enlarge my tent by building bigger barns. After my tithe, I'll be able to take life easy, eat, drink, and be merry!'

And so, he lived off of his riches until his old age.

This is how it will be for those whom God has blessed. They will have an easy and abundant life just like the Son of Man who has many homes to lay His head and earns a lucrative income from His ministry."

Mt 13:1-23; Mk 4:1-20; Lk 8:1-15
Parable of the Sower

A farmer walked down a path through the centre of his field scattering seed to the left and right of the path. However, the seeds on the left criticised those on the right; and those on the right criticised those on the left. To each, the other was clearly not of the farmer's field and so couldn't be part of his crop.

The seeds used so much energy criticising each other that their growth was severely stunted.

Whoever has ears, listen!

Perfect Parables

What would it be like if all the characters in the parables made the right choices?

Lk 18:1-8
The Persistent Widow

Jesus told his disciples a parable to show their need to be persistent in prayer and never quit. He said, "There was a judge in a town who neither feared God nor cared about people. A widow in that town kept at him: 'Grant me justice against my adversary.' She also prayed for the judge to have a change of heart. At first the judge ignored her, but eventually, her prayers began to see a softening in his heart.

The judge summoned the widow, 'I'm sorry for putting you off. I was wrong. Let me right this wrong and ensure you get justice.'"

Then Jesus said, "If an evil judge can be transformed by the grace of God, there is hope for even the worst of sinners. Keep calling on the mighty name of God who holds the hearts of kings in his hands like a stream of water that he channels towards all who please him."

Lk 18:9-14
The Pharisee and the Tax Collector

Then he told this parable to those who were confident in their own righteousness and who looked down on everyone else.

Two men went to the Temple to pray, one a Pharisee, the other a tax collector. The Pharisee prayed with his face in his hands: 'God, have mercy on me, a sinner. I have limited your mercy to those whom I thought deserved it, and yet grace is a gift. Thank you that you welcome all, no matter where they come from, especially that tax collector over there!'

The tax collector also prayed with his face in his hands and said, 'God have mercy on me, a sinner. For not only have I betrayed my people, but I have judged the Pharisees because they make me more aware of my current state.'

I tell you that both the Pharisee and tax collector went home right with God. For the humble shall be raised up and the dividing wall shall be broken down."

Mt 21:28-32
The Two Sons

"What do you think about this? A man had two sons. He went to the first and said, 'Son, go and work in the vineyard today.'

The son answered, 'I will.' He headed out right away.

Before the father even asked the other son, the boy piped up and said, 'Don't worry father, I'll go too.' He soon joined his brother in the vineyard.

Which of the two sons did what the father wanted?"

"Both," they answered.

Jesus said to them, "I tell you that God's Kingdom is wider than you can imagine."

Mt:21:33-44; Mk 12:1-12; Lk 20:9-18
The Wicked Tenants

Jesus spoke to them in parables. "A man planted a vineyard. He put a wall around it, dug a pit for the winepress, and built a watchman's tower. Then he leased it out to some tenant farmers and went away. At harvest time, he sent a servant to collect his share of the crop.

The tenants gladly complied, but the harvest was so bountiful that they needed many more servants to help. The owner was so delighted that he sent his beloved son to thank them personally.

When the tenants saw him coming, they rejoiced, 'This is the heir! How blessed are we to be honoured with his visit!' They welcomed him with open arms, threw a party, and then gave him a grand tour of all they had done to with the vineyard.

"What do you think the owner will do when hears what happened? He will give those tenants an inheritance as well."

Pointless Parables

Just for a little light hearted fun...

Mk 4:21-25; Lk 8:16-18
The Lamp on a Stand

Someone lit a lamp and then set it upon a lamp stand. Now he could read.

Mt 18:21-35
The Unforgiving Servant

Then Peter came to Jesus and asked, "Master, how many times should I forgive my brother who sinned against me? The other rabbis say I should forgive him three times. You are more holy than they. Should it be seven times, the number of perfection?"

Jesus replied, "Not seven times but seventy times seven"

Peter exclaimed, "But, it's Monopoly."

"Well, why didn't you say so in the first place? Then even three times is way too many!"

Lk 15:11-32
The Prodigal Son

A man had two sons. The younger said to his father, 'Father, give me my share of the estate now, instead of making me wait until you die.' So the Father divided his property between them.

Soon after, the younger son packed all he had and set off for a distant country. There he squandered his money in wild living until it was all gone. At that time, there was a great famine and he began to starve. The only job he could find was feeding a Gentile farmer's pigs. The boy became so hungry that he wanted to eat the pig swill.

When he finally came to his senses, he said, 'At home, even my father's servants have food to spare, and here I am starving to death! I will go home to my father and say, 'Father, I've sinned against God and against you. I am no longer worthy to be called your son. Take me on as a hired servant.'

And so, he got up and headed home to his father. But while he was still a long way off, his father saw him and was filled with compassion. He ran to his son, embraced him in his arms, and showered him with kisses. The son began his speech, 'Father, I have sinned against God and against you. I am no longer worthy to be called your son – "

But his father cut him off and said to his servants, 'Quick! Bring the finest robe and put it on him. Put the family ring on his finger and place sandals on his feet. Get the fattened calf and kill it. Let's celebrate and have a feast. For this son of mine was dead and is alive again. He was lost and is found.'

However, the fattened calf realised that his 'invitation' to the celebration was not to be as a guest, and so he quickly set off for a distant country. And though the Father looked for him every day, he never did return.

Mt 25:14-30; Lk 19:11-27
Parable of the Talents

"The Kingdom of heaven is like a man going on a journey who called his servants together and entrusted his pet rabbits to them. To the first he gave five rabbits, to the second two rabbits and to the third one rabbit, each in proportion to his ability. Then he left on his journey.

"The first servant immediately put his rabbits together in a pen and soon gained five more. So too, the second servant gained two more. But the last servant couldn't seem to get any more rabbits no matter how hard he tried."

Lk 16:1-12
The Shrewd Manager

Jesus told this story to his disciples, "There was a rich man who had a manager who handled his affairs. However, he heard reports that the manager was lining his own pockets. So he summoned him and asked, 'What's this I hear about you? Don't you know that it's the tailor's job to do that?'

The LOST Parables

Allegorical tales that speak straight to the heart.

The Band Who Didn't Play

Once, there was a band whose purpose was to play beautiful music to bless the community. They would meet on a Sunday to practise and then perform in the town centre during the following week.

Although the band could see they were a blessing to others, they realised they would play even better if they had someone to help them keep time. And so, the group duly elected the one member of the band who they all felt had the best sense of timing to be a conductor. He directed their playing to ensure it was their very best.

The community appreciated the difference and would clap and cheer. The conductor would move out the way and let the band receive the applause. His job was to help the band play their best.

But something happened over time.

At first, it started small.

Whereas before, everyone took responsibility for themselves, the band began to expect that the conductor would organise the practise times and ensure their attendance at the performance, as he was the one "in charge."

As the band started taking less responsibility, the conductor began to feel he had to be the one reprimanding those who weren't pulling their weight, making sure they were playing their best. Since he was the one holding it all together, he would bow first at performances, *then* signal for the band to take a bow.

The band soon perceived the role of the conductor as the most important. They forgot that it was they who made the music, whereas the conductor's duty was only to conduct their playing. They would turn up for the concert during the week and occasionally attend practises, but they couldn't be bothered to do anything outside of these times. Some felt that turning up and watching the conductor was "doing their bit" and stopped playing altogether!

Some wanted to do the most important job and asked if they could conduct. When not conducting, the would-be conductors spent their time silently judging the conductor's technique. As they felt they could do better, they only played half-heartedly; if they played at all, that is. Others interrupted both the practises and the performances to advise the conductor as to how he could do his job better!

Eventually, a couple of band members became resentful at their conductor's inferior performance. Combined with their frustration at the perceived lack of opportunity to conduct, they decided to form their own band, and made sure they were in charge. These new conductors would then tell everyone else how they were the *real* band and encourage other players to join them and informed audiences that they should only attend their performances.

Some women in the band disliked that the conductor was male. They spent less time playing and more time complaining about how it was unfair and sexist. They asserted, therefore, that the band wouldn't include the whole community. Some of the disgruntled women broke away and formed their splinter band with a female conductor. They too spent their time explaining how they were the *real* band, the other bands were all wrong, and *their* band would most bless the public as a result.

Still others felt that the band wasn't inclusive enough. They spent less time playing and more time complaining that people who didn't play any instruments weren't welcome into the band. Eventually, that faction formed their own splinter "band" of non-musical members. They were convinced the general population would appreciate their non-musical group as its membership comprised of people just like them.

All too soon, all weekly performances became complete farces. Bands competed to gain attention from the public, stridently proclaiming that *their* music was the right music and everyone else's music was inferior at best. Spats between the various conductors became public. Little music was actually being played. Less and less band members turned up for performances. Those that did show up either didn't play, or they interrupted their conductors to tell them how it should really be done.

And so, the community was no longer blessed. As a result, people grew to see that music was irrelevant. There were even some in the community who campaigned to disallow bands "playing" in public altogether. But to be honest, most outside the bands merely saw music as meaningless drivel and never bothered to listen to what the bands called "performances". The younger folk felt such things were apparently only for the older generation who attended out of a misguided duty and as such couldn't see it for the absurdity it was.

Other "Lost Parables" are available as eBooks on Amazon with illustrations. Suitable for use in all age church services, family devotions, Sunday school or for reading to your children or to yourself.

NOT the Beginning

A clever section title that makes it sound like it's more important than 'all the stuff that goes at the end of a book'...

Get Bonus Content

Subscribers to my mailing list will receive a free eBook or audiobook of *"Not the Parable of the Lost Sheep"* and, if you stick around you'll also receive *"Not the Parable of the Rich Fool"*. Twenty satirical takes on this parable not available anywhere else.

www.johnspencerwrites.com/signup

In addition you'll also receive:

- an email every Friday(ish) chock full of the week's memes I put out on social media
- details of the monthly competitions where you can win signed copies of my books
- notifications of all promotional deals on my books
- opportunities to beta read and receive free review copies
- the satisfaction of making John feel loved and wanted.

Alternatively, if you'd just like to know when I'm releasing new books then feel free to sign up, grab the first freebie, unsubscribe, then follow me on Amazon, Goodreads or BookBub.

Feedback

If this book has made you think or laugh or both, then it would mean so much to me if you would leave a review on Amazon and Goodreads even if it's only a sentence.

I appreciate that writing a review takes time, so please feel free to use my insta-review-maker™ below:

This book was poignant/prosaic/putrescent!

I was up all night thinking/reading another book instead/cleaning my mind.

My favourite bit was how I realised I was laughing at me/when I stopped reading it/when I poured bleach all over it.

I recommend that you replace your preacher with it/read a funnier book/call the sanitation department.

About the Author

John was born at a very young age with his umbilical cord wrapped around his neck. At first, it appeared that no lasting damage had been done, but as he grew, it became clear that his sense of humour had been damaged irreparably.

Not even Bible College, counselling, and prayer ministry has been able to rectify things, so John eagerly awaits the new creation where his humour will be perfected.

John also trained as a teacher at Oxford University, but despite this he still refers to himself in the third person. Whilst there, he performed stand-up comedy as part of the Oxford Revue but got tired and has been sitting down at his desk to perform his humour ever since.

So now, when he's not wrestling with work-life balance or literally wrestling with his four children, he's wrestling with writing funny words on a page in his cramped study.

John lives with his family near Oxford, England where daily he wonders how his wife still finds the same jokes funny after more than 20 years of marriage.

Keep in touch

Mailing list – did I mention that you can sign up and receive bonus eBooks/audiobooks?

www.johnspencerwrites.com/signup

Just thought I'd remind you. You know, just in case.

Amazon, Goodreads and Bookbub

You can follow me on these and apparently they will let you know when I publish new books.

Social media

You can find me on **Facebook, Twitter,** and now, **Pinterest**[*]. I'll be wearing glasses, a red and white stripped sweater, and woolly hat whilst posting memes daily.

I'm most active on **Twitter** exchanging banter with the rest of the Christian anon gang.

And you're least likely to see my humorous memes on Facebook unless you choose "See First" under the "Liked"

---

[*] Though still not Instagram, as my children still haven't explained to me how this works.

menu on my page. If the thought of that makes you sad, then you know what to do.

Blog

I blog occasionally on my website at:

        www.johnspencerwrites.com

And I write Christian satirical news at:

        www.saltycee.com

Other books by the author

After reading this book you might be tempted to check out my other books to see if they're any better. By the Law of Averages, you're sure to eventually find something that will make you laugh.

If not, then why not think of your purchase as helping keep me off of the streets where my humour could cause some serious harm to innocent bystanders.

Not the Bible Titles

Alternative takes on the original parables to snap us out of our over-familiarity and open our eyes to the truth of the Gospel.

Not the Parables of Jesus

Not the Parable of the Good Samaritan

Still More Not the Parables of Jesus

Not the Parable of the Lost Sheep *(free for subscribers)*

Not the Parable of the Rich Fool *(subscribers only)*

Not the Christmas Story Vol 1 *(with devotional)*

Christian Parody Titles
Not the Love Dare
Because everyone needs some biblical help to justify their annoying habits to their spouse

Not the Christmas Story: A Comedic Christmas Caper
"Fear not: for, behold, I bring you good tidings of great laughter, which shall be to all purchasers of this book."

Christian Satirical News Titles
The Best of the Salty Cee Vol 1
News Satire more salty than the Dead Sea.

Lost Parable Series
Short allegorical tales available as ebooks with illustrations for the young and the young at heart.

The Donkey and the King

Ana and the Prince

The Princess and the Crocodile

Satirical Self-Publishing titles
Get 1000 readers for your self-published book
Love it or hate it, it's the Marmite of marketing books.

Kingdom Collective Publishing

Kingdom Collective Publishing welcomes others who want to join together to bless, encourage, and help build up the Body of Christ so that we all attain the whole measure of the fullness of Christ.

We're not about building ministries or making money. We're about using our gifts to sow into the Kingdom and bring transformation.

This book has finished.

No, really, it's finished.

Look, it's not like a performance where you get an encore.

OK, I admit your persistence is admirable.

Oh go on then:

A tree and its fruit
You can tell a tree by its fruit. If it's got fruit then it's a tree. Unless it's blackberries or strawberries, then it's a bush.

Satisfied?

Now how about that nice review?

www.ingramcontent.com/pod-product-compliance
Lightning Source LLC
Chambersburg PA
CBHW071019080526
44587CB00015B/2424